For C, B♭, E♭ & Bass Clef Instruments

CHRISTMAS TUNES

Play-Along

Recorded by Ric Probst at Tanner Monagle Studio
Tenor Sax: Eric Schoor
Piano: Mark Davis
Bass: Jeff Hamann
Drums: David Bayles

To access online content, visit:
www.halleonard.com/mylibrary

**Enter Code
8733-2512-1421-9269**

ISBN 978-1-5400-2944-7

HAL•LEONARD®

For more information on the Real Book series, including community forums, please visit
www.OfficialRealBook.com

Visit Hal Leonard Online at
www.halleonard.com

Contact Us:
Hal Leonard
7777 West Bluemound Road
Milwaukee, WI 53213
Email: info@halleonard.com

In Europe contact:
Hal Leonard Europe Limited
Distribution Centre, Newmarket Road
Bury St Edmunds, Suffolk, IP33 3YB
Email: info@halleonardeurope.com

In Australia contact:
Hal Leonard Australia Pty. Ltd.
4 Lentara Court
Cheltenham, Victoria, 3192 Australia
Email: info@halleonard.com.au

Contents

THE CHRISTMAS SONG
(CHESTNUTS ROASTING ON AN OPEN FIRE)

— MEL TORME/ROBERT WELLS

C VERSION

(BALLAD)

FINE AFTER SOLO,
D.C. AL FINE

DO YOU HEAR WHAT I HEAR

— NOEL REGNEY/GLORIA SHAYNE

C VERSION

(MED. SLOW)

REPEAT HEAD IN/OUT
AFTER SOLOS, D.S. AL ⊕
(PLAY PICKUPS) (TAKE REPEAT)

6

FELIZ NAVIDAD

– JOSÉ FELICIANO

C VERSION

(FAST LATIN)

FINE

AFTER SOLOS, D.S. AL FINE
(PLAY PICKUPS) (TAKE REPEAT)

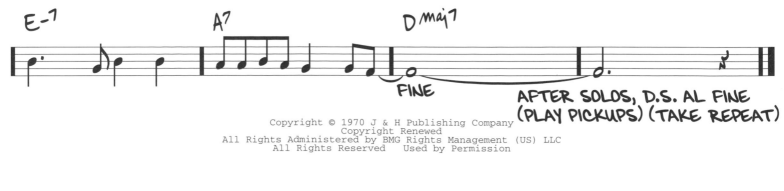

HERE COMES SANTA CLAUS
(RIGHT DOWN SANTA CLAUS LANE)

– GENE AUTRY/OAKLEY HALDEMAN

(UP SWING)

C VERSION

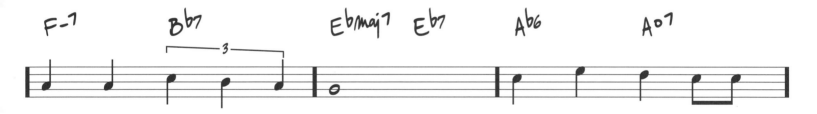

Fine

REPEAT HEAD IN/OUT
AFTER SOLOS, D.C. AL FINE

8

A HOLLY JOLLY CHRISTMAS

– JOHNNY MARKS

C VERSION

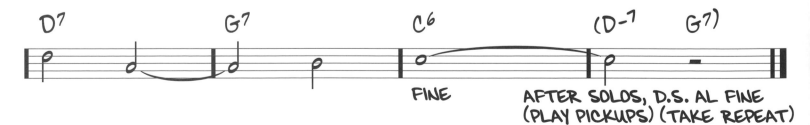

FINE

AFTER SOLOS, D.S. AL FINE
(PLAY PICKUPS) (TAKE REPEAT)

LET IT SNOW! LET IT SNOW! LET IT SNOW!

(MED. SWING)

— SAMMY CAHN/JULE STYNE

C VERSION

FINE
AFTER SOLOS, D.S. AL FINE
(PLAY PICKUPS) (TAKE REPEAT)

THE LITTLE DRUMMER BOY

- Harry Simeone/Henry Onorati/Katherine Davis

C Version

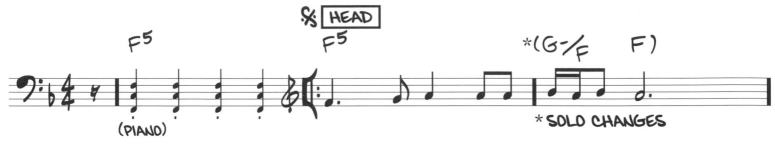

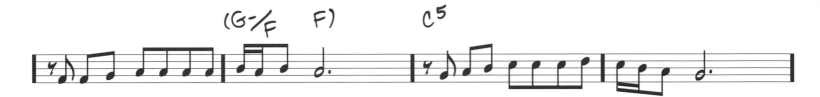

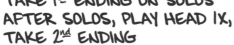

REPEAT HEAD IN
TAKE 1st ENDING ON SOLOS
AFTER SOLOS, PLAY HEAD 1x,
TAKE 2nd ENDING

12
(UP WALTZ)

THE MOST WONDERFUL TIME OF THE YEAR

— EDDIE POLA/GEORGE WYLE

C VERSION

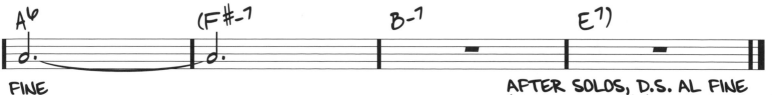

FINE

AFTER SOLOS, D.S. AL FINE
(PLAY PICKUPS) (TAKE REPEAT)

SLEIGH RIDE

— LEROY ANDERSON

(MED. TWO BEAT)

C VERSION

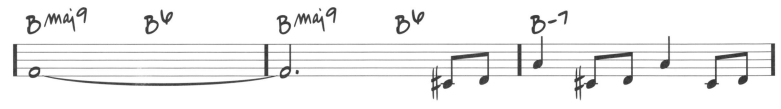

AFTER SOLO, D.S. AL FINE
(PLAY PICKUPS) (TAKE REPEATS)

Do You Hear What I Hear

- Noel Regney/Gloria Shayne

(MED. SLOW)

Bb Version

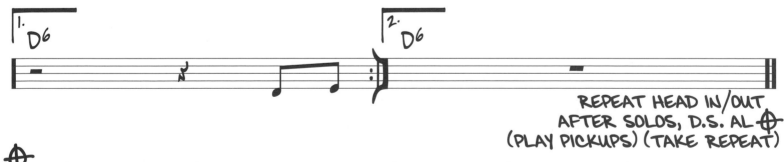

REPEAT HEAD IN/OUT
AFTER SOLOS, D.S. AL ⊕
(PLAY PICKUPS) (TAKE REPEAT)

FELIZ NAVIDAD

– JOSÉ FELICIANO

Here Comes Santa Claus
(Right Down Santa Claus Lane)

- Gene Autry/Oakley Haldeman

(UP SWING)

Bb Version

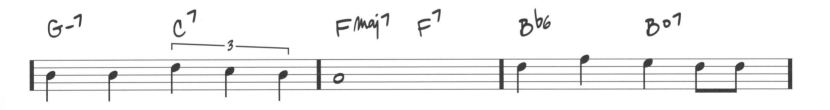

FINE
REPEAT HEAD IN/OUT
AFTER SOLOS, D.C. AL FINE

A HOLLY JOLLY CHRISTMAS

— JOHNNY MARKS

Bb Version

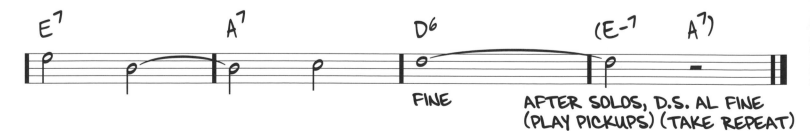

FINE

AFTER SOLOS, D.S. AL FINE
(PLAY PICKUPS) (TAKE REPEAT)

LET IT SNOW! LET IT SNOW! LET IT SNOW!

(MED. SWING)

— SAMMY CAHN/JULE STYNE

Bb VERSION

FINE
AFTER SOLOS, D.S. AL FINE
(PLAY PICKUPS) (TAKE REPEAT)

THE LITTLE DRUMMER BOY

— Harry Simeone/Henry Onorati/Katherine Davis

Bb Version

(SLOW)

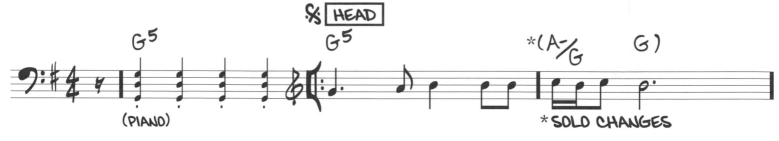

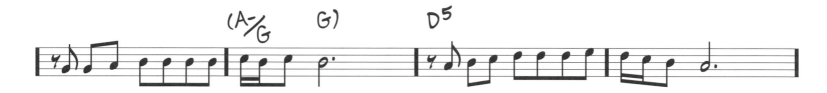

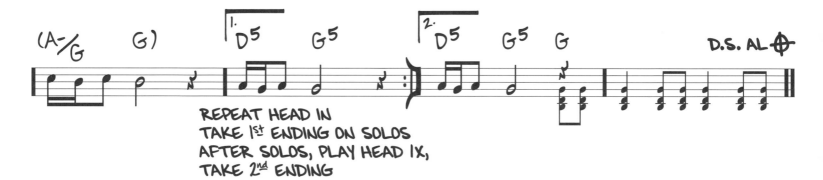

REPEAT HEAD IN
TAKE 1ST ENDING ON SOLOS
AFTER SOLOS, PLAY HEAD 1X,
TAKE 2ND ENDING

RUDOLPH THE RED-NOSED REINDEER

(MED. FAST SWING)

- JOHNNY MARKS

Bb Version

FINE

D.S. FOR SOLOS
AFTER SOLOS, D.S. AL FINE
(TAKE REPEAT)

24
(UP WALTZ)
THE MOST WONDERFUL TIME OF THE YEAR

- EDDIE POLA/GEORGE WYLE

Bb VERSION

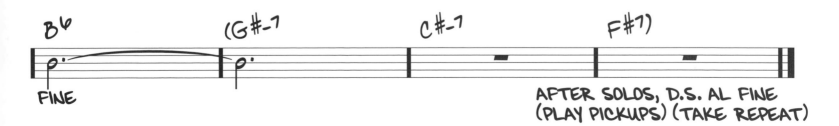

FINE

AFTER SOLOS, D.S. AL FINE
(PLAY PICKUPS) (TAKE REPEAT)

Sleigh Ride

- Leroy Anderson

AFTER SOLO, D.S. AL FINE
(PLAY PICKUPS) (TAKE REPEATS)

THE CHRISTMAS SONG
(CHESTNUTS ROASTING ON AN OPEN FIRE)

(BALLAD)

Eb Version

– MEL TORME/ROBERT WELLS

FINE AFTER SOLO,
D.C. AL FINE

Do You Hear What I Hear

- Noel Regney/Gloria Shayne

Eb Version

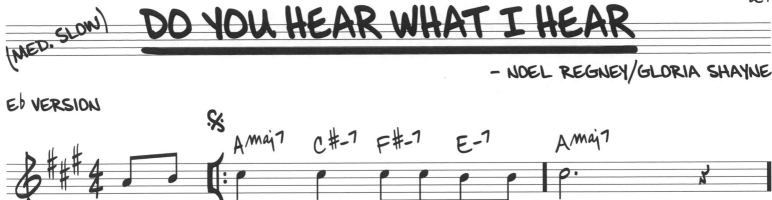
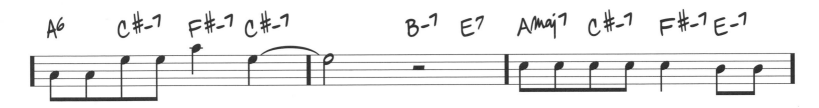

REPEAT HEAD IN/OUT
AFTER SOLOS, D.S. AL ⊕
(PLAY PICKUPS) (TAKE REPEAT)

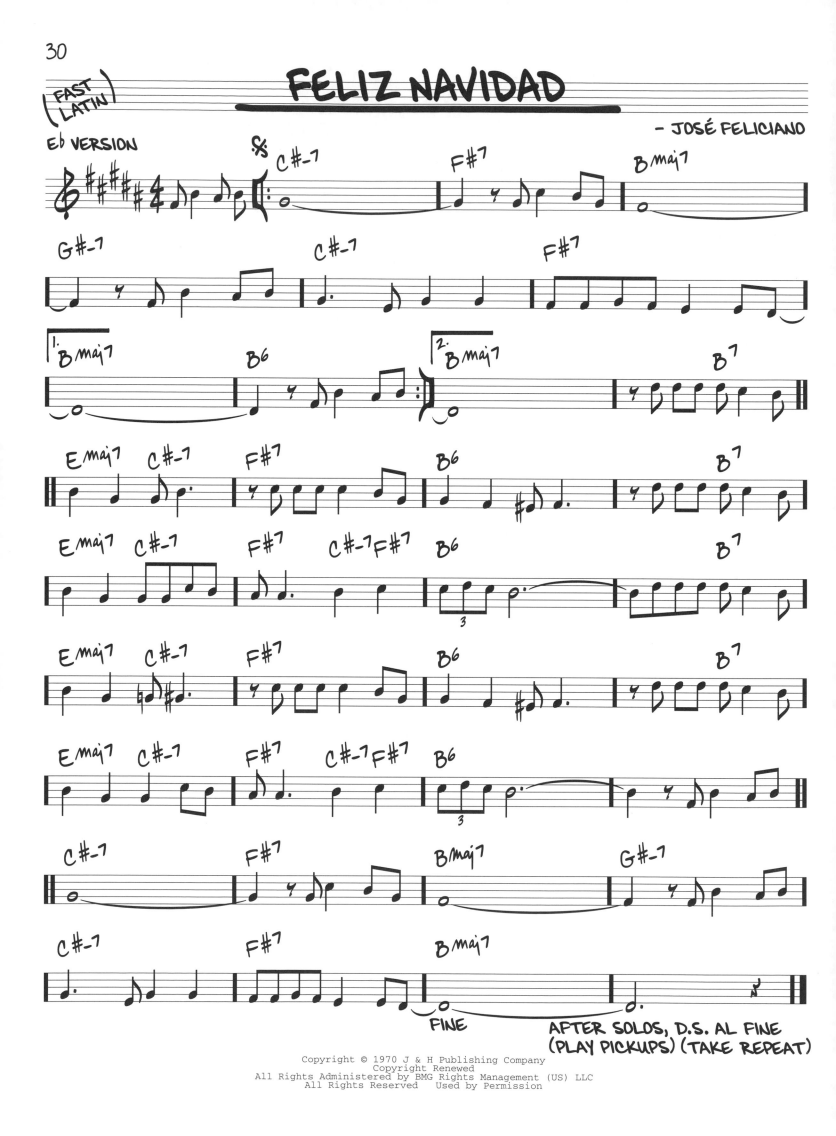

Feliz Navidad

HERE COMES SANTA CLAUS
(RIGHT DOWN SANTA CLAUS LANE)

- Gene Autry/Oakley Haldeman

(UP SWING)

Eb VERSION

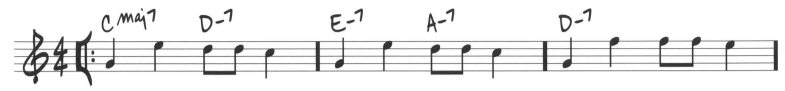

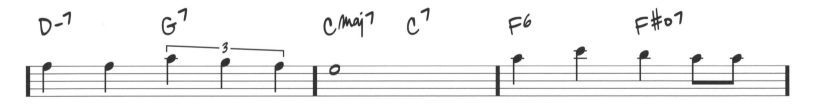

FINE
REPEAT HEAD IN/OUT
AFTER SOLOS, D.C. AL FINE

A HOLLY JOLLY CHRISTMAS

– JOHNNY MARKS

Eb VERSION

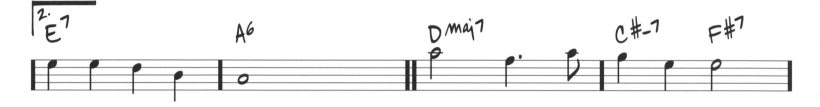

FINE

AFTER SOLOS, D.S. AL FINE
(PLAY PICKUPS) (TAKE REPEAT)

LET IT SNOW! LET IT SNOW! LET IT SNOW!

(MED. SWING)

Eb VERSION

— SAMMY CAHN/JULE STYNE

FINE
AFTER SOLOS, D.S. AL FINE
(PLAY PICKUPS) (TAKE REPEAT)

THE LITTLE DRUMMER BOY

- Harry Simeone/Henry Onorati/Katherine Davis

Eb Version

REPEAT HEAD IN
TAKE 1st ENDING ON SOLOS
AFTER SOLOS, PLAY HEAD 1x,
TAKE 2nd ENDING

RUDOLPH THE RED-NOSED REINDEER

- Johnny Marks

FINE

D.S. FOR SOLOS
AFTER SOLOS, D.S. AL FINE
(TAKE REPEAT)

36

(UP WALTZ)

THE MOST WONDERFUL TIME OF THE YEAR

- EDDIE POLA/GEORGE WYLE

Eb Version

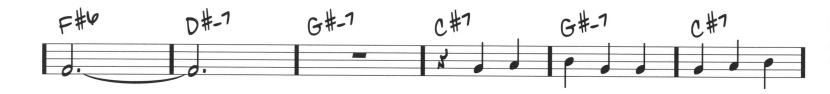

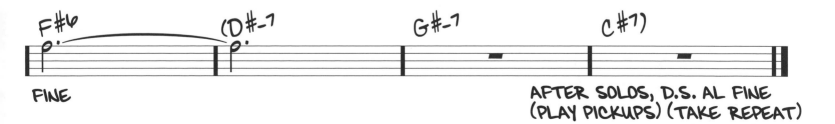

FINE

AFTER SOLOS, D.S. AL FINE
(PLAY PICKUPS) (TAKE REPEAT)

Sleigh Ride

- Leroy Anderson

Do You Hear What I Hear

- Noel Regney/Gloria Shayne

(Med. Slow)

C Bass Version

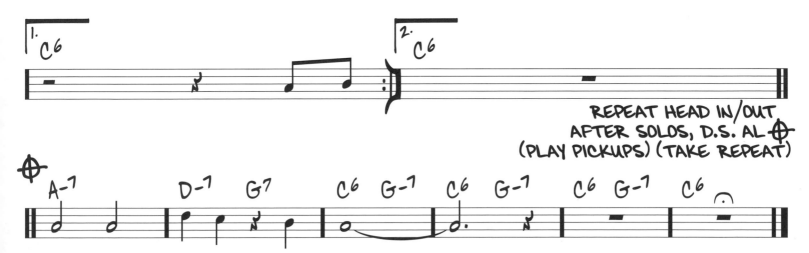

Repeat Head In/Out
After Solos, D.S. al ⨁
(Play Pickups) (Take Repeat)

42

Feliz Navidad

— José Feliciano

(FAST LATIN)

C BASS VERSION

FINE

AFTER SOLOS, D.S. AL FINE
(PLAY PICKUPS) (TAKE REPEAT)

HERE COMES SANTA CLAUS
(RIGHT DOWN SANTA CLAUS LANE)

- Gene Autry/Oakley Haldeman

C BASS VERSION

(UP SWING)

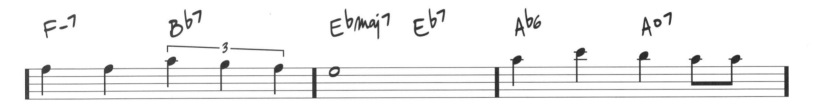

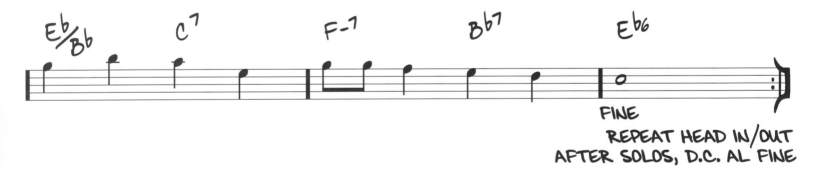

FINE
REPEAT HEAD IN/OUT
AFTER SOLOS, D.C. AL FINE

A HOLLY JOLLY CHRISTMAS

C BASS VERSION

— JOHNNY MARKS

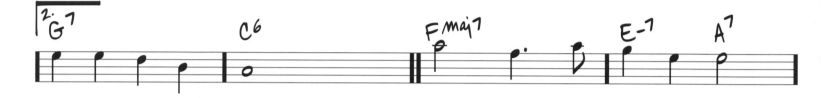

FINE

AFTER SOLOS, D.S. AL FINE
(PLAY PICKUPS) (TAKE REPEAT)

LET IT SNOW! LET IT SNOW! LET IT SNOW!

— SAMMY CAHN/JULE STYNE

C BASS VERSION

FINE
AFTER SOLOS, D.S. AL FINE
(PLAY PICKUPS) (TAKE REPEAT)

THE LITTLE DRUMMER BOY

- Harry Simeone/Henry Onorati/Katherine Davis

C BASS VERSION

REPEAT HEAD IN
TAKE 1ST ENDING ON SOLOS
AFTER SOLOS, PLAY HEAD 1X,
TAKE 2ND ENDING

RUDOLPH THE RED-NOSED REINDEER

(MED. FAST SWING)

– JOHNNY MARKS

C BASS VERSION

FINE

D.S. FOR SOLOS
AFTER SOLOS, D.S. AL FINE
(TAKE REPEAT)

THE MOST WONDERFUL TIME OF THE YEAR

- EDDIE POLA/GEORGE WYLE

(UP WALTZ)

C BASS VERSION

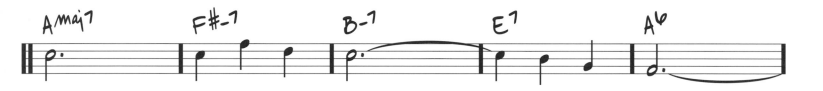

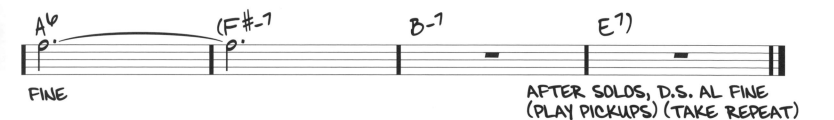

FINE

AFTER SOLOS, D.S. AL FINE
(PLAY PICKUPS) (TAKE REPEAT)

SLEIGH RIDE

— LEROY ANDERSON

(MED. TWO BEAT)

C BASS VERSION

LAST X, TO ⊕

AFTER SOLO, D.S. AL FINE
(PLAY PICKUPS) (TAKE REPEATS)

THE REAL BOOK MULTI-TRACKS

TODAY'S BEST WAY TO PRACTICE JAZZ!

Accurate, easy-to-read lead sheets and professional, customizable audio tracks accessed online for 10 songs.

1. MAIDEN VOYAGE PLAY-ALONG

Autumn Leaves • Blue Bossa • Doxy • Footprints • Maiden Voyage • Now's the Time • On Green Dolphin Street • Satin Doll • Summertime • Tune Up.
00196616 Book with Online Media...$17.99

2. MILES DAVIS PLAY-ALONG

Blue in Green • Boplicity (Be Bop Lives) • Four • Freddie Freeloader • Milestones • Nardis • Seven Steps to Heaven • So What • Solar • Walkin'.
00196798 Book with Online Media...$17.99

3. ALL BLUES PLAY-ALONG

All Blues • Back at the Chicken Shack • Billie's Bounce (Bill's Bounce) • Birk's Works • Blues by Five • C-Jam Blues • Mr. P.C. • One for Daddy-O • Reunion Blues • Turnaround.
00196692 Book with Online Media...$17.99

4. CHARLIE PARKER PLAY-ALONG

Anthropology • Blues for Alice • Confirmation • Donna Lee • K.C. Blues • Moose the Mooche • My Little Suede Shoes • Ornithology • Scrapple from the Apple • Yardbird Suite.
00196799 Book with Online Media...$17.99

5. JAZZ FUNK PLAY-ALONG

Alligator Bogaloo • The Chicken • Cissy Strut • Cold Duck Time • Comin' Home Baby • Mercy, Mercy, Mercy • Put It Where You Want It • Sidewinder • Tom Cat • Watermelon Man.
00196728 Book with Online Media...$17.99

6. SONNY ROLLINS PLAY-ALONG

Airegin • Blue Seven • Doxy • Duke of Iron • Oleo • Pent up House • St. Thomas • Sonnymoon for Two • Strode Rode • Tenor Madness.
00218264 Book with Online Media...$17.99

7. THELONIOUS MONK PLAY-ALONG

Bemsha Swing • Blue Monk • Bright Mississippi • Green Chimneys • Monk's Dream • Reflections • Rhythm-a-ning • 'Round Midnight • Straight No Chaser • Ugly Beauty.
00232768 Book with Online Media...$17.99

8. BEBOP ERA PLAY-ALONG

Au Privave • Boneology • Bouncing with Bud • Dexterity • Groovin' High • Half Nelson • In Walked Bud • Lady Bird • Move • Witches Pit.
00196728 Book with Online Media...$17.99

9. CHRISTMAS CLASSICS PLAY-ALONG

Blue Christmas • Christmas Time Is Here • Frosty the Snow Man • Have Yourself a Merry Little Christmas • I'll Be Home for Christmas • My Favorite Things • Santa Claus Is Comin' to Town • Silver Bells • White Christmas • Winter Wonderland.
00236808 Book with Online Media...$17.99

10. CHRISTMAS SONGS PLAY-ALONG

Away in a Manger • The First Noel • Go, Tell It on the Mountain • Hark! the Herald Angels Sing • Jingle Bells • Joy to the World • O Come, All Ye Faithful • O Holy Night • Up on the Housetop • We Wish You a Merry Christmas.
00236809 Book with Online Media...$17.99

15. CHRISTMAS TUNES PLAY-ALONG

The Christmas Song (Chestnuts Roasting on an Open Fire) • Do You Hear What I Hear • Feliz Navidad • Here Comes Santa Claus (Right down Santa Claus Lane) • A Holly Jolly Christmas • Let It Snow! Let It Snow! Let It Snow! • The Little Drummer Boy • The Most Wonderful Time of the Year • Rudolph the Red-Nosed Reindeer • Sleigh Ride.
00278073 Book with Online Media...$17.99

www.halleonard.com

0718

The Best-Selling Jazz Book of All Time Is Now Legal!

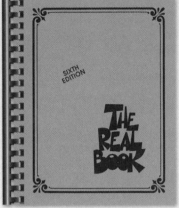

The Real Books are the most popular jazz books of all time. Since the 1970s, musicians have trusted these volumes to get them through every gig, night after night. The problem is that the books were illegally produced and distributed, without any regard to copyright law, or royalties paid to the composers who created these musical masterpieces.

Hal Leonard is very proud to present the first legitimate and legal editions of these books ever produced. You won't even notice the difference, other than all the notorious errors being fixed: the covers and typeface look the same, the song lists are nearly identical, and the price for our edition is even cheaper than the originals!

Every conscientious musician will appreciate that these books are now produced accurately and ethically, benefitting the songwriters that we owe for some of the greatest tunes of all time!

VOLUME 1
00240221	C Edition	$39.99
00240224	B♭ Edition	$39.99
00240225	E♭ Edition	$39.99
00240226	Bass Clef Edition	$39.99
00240292	C Edition 6 x 9	$35.00
00240339	B♭ Edition 6 x 9	$35.00
00147792	Bass Clef Edition 6 x 9	$35.00
00451087	C Edition on CD-ROM	$29.99
00200984	Online Backing Tracks: Selections	$45.00
00110604	Book/USB Flash Drive Backing Tracks Pack	$79.99
00110599	USB Flash Drive Only	$50.00

VOLUME 2
00240222	C Edition	$39.99
00240227	B♭ Edition	$39.99
00240228	E♭ Edition	$39.99
00240229	Bass Clef Edition	$39.99
00240293	C Edition 6 x 9	$35.00
00125900	B♭ Edition 6 x 9	$35.00
00451088	C Edition on CD-ROM	$30.99
00125900	The Real Book – Mini Edition	$35.00
00204126	Backing Tracks on USB Flash Drive	$50.00
00204131	C Edition – USB Flash Drive Pack	$79.99

VOLUME 3
00240233	C Edition	$39.99
00240284	B♭ Edition	$39.99
00240285	E♭ Edition	$39.99
00240286	Bass Clef Edition	$39.99
00240338	C Edition 6 x 9	$35.00
00451089	C Edition on CD-ROM	$29.99

VOLUME 4
00240296	C Edition	$39.99
00103348	B♭ Edition	$39.99
00103349	E♭ Edition	$39.99
00103350	Bass Clef Edition	$39.99

VOLUME 5
00240349	C Edition	$39.99
00175278	B♭ Edition	$39.99
00175279	E♭ Edition	$39.99

VOLUME 6
00240534	C Edition	$39.99
00223637	E♭ Edition	$39.99

Also available:
00154230	The Real Bebop Book	$34.99
00240264	The Real Blues Book	$34.99
00310910	The Real Bluegrass Book	$32.50
00240223	The Real Broadway Book	$35.00
00240440	The Trane Book	$22.99
00125426	The Real Country Book	$39.99
00240355	The Real Dixieland Book C Edition	$32.50
00122335	The Real Dixieland Book B♭ Edition	$32.50
00240235	The Duke Ellington Real Book	$19.99
00240268	The Real Jazz Solos Book	$30.00
00240348	The Real Latin Book C Edition	$37.50
00127107	The Real Latin Book B♭ Edition	$35.00
00120809	The Pat Metheny Real Book C Edition	$27.50
00252119	The Pat Metheny Real Book B♭ Edition	$24.99
00240358	The Charlie Parker Real Book	$19.99
00118324	The Real Pop Book – Vol. 1	$35.00
00240331	The Bud Powell Real Book	$19.99
00240437	The Real R&B Book	$39.99
00240313	The Real Rock Book	$35.00
00240323	The Real Rock Book – Vol. 2	$35.00
00240359	The Real Tab Book	$32.50
00240317	The Real Worship Book	$29.99

THE REAL CHRISTMAS BOOK
00240306	C Edition	$32.50
00240345	B♭ Edition	$32.50
00240346	E♭ Edition	$32.50
00240347	Bass Clef Edition	$32.50
00240431	A-G CD Backing Tracks	$24.99
00240432	H-M CD Backing Tracks	$24.99
00240433	N-Y CD Backing Tracks	$24.99

THE REAL VOCAL BOOK
00240230	Volume 1 High Voice	$35.00
00240307	Volume 1 Low Voice	$35.00
00240231	Volume 2 High Voice	$35.00
00240308	Volume 2 Low Voice	$35.00
00240391	Volume 3 High Voice	$35.00
00240392	Volume 3 Low Voice	$35.00
00118318	Volume 4 High Voice	$35.00
00118319	Volume 4 Low Voice	$35.00

THE REAL BOOK – STAFF PAPER
00240327	$10.99

HOW TO PLAY FROM A REAL BOOK
00312097	$17.50

THE REAL BOOK – ENHANCED CHORDS
00151290	$29.99

Complete song lists online at www.halleonard.com

Prices, content, and availability subject to change without notice.

0718

For use with all B-flat, E-flat, Bass Clef and C instruments, the Jazz Play-Along® Series is the ultimate learning tool for all jazz musicians. With musician-friendly lead sheets, melody cues, and other split-track audio choices included, these first-of-a-kind packages help you master improvisation while playing some of the greatest tunes of all time. FOR STUDY, each tune includes a split track with: melody cue with proper style and inflection • professional rhythm tracks • choruses for soloing • removable bass part • removable piano part. FOR PERFORMANCE, each tune also has: an additional full stereo accompaniment track (no melody) • additional choruses for soloing.

90. THELONIOUS MONK CLASSICS 00841262 ....$16.99	**125. SAMMY NESTICO** 00843187 ....$16.99	**160. GEORGE SHEARING** 14041531 ....$16.99
91. THELONIOUS MONK FAVORITES 00841263 ....$16.99	**126. COUNT BASIE CLASSICS** 00843157 ....$16.99	**161. DAVE BRUBECK** 14041556 ....$16.99
92. LEONARD BERNSTEIN 00450134 ....$16.99	**127. CHUCK MANGIONE** 00843188 ....$16.99	**162. BIG CHRISTMAS COLLECTION** 00843221 ....$24.99
93. DISNEY FAVORITES 00843142 ....$16.99	**128. VOCAL STANDARDS (LOW VOICE)** 00843189 ....$16.99	**163. JOHN COLTRANE STANDARDS** 00843235 ....$16.99
94. RAY 00843143 ....$16.99	**129. VOCAL STANDARDS (HIGH VOICE)** 00843190 ....$16.99	**164. HERB ALPERT** 14041775 ....$16.99
95. JAZZ AT THE LOUNGE 00843144 ....$16.99	**130. VOCAL JAZZ (LOW VOICE)** 00843191 ....$16.99	**165. GEORGE BENSON** 00843240 ....$16.99
96. LATIN JAZZ STANDARDS 00843145 ....$16.99	**131. VOCAL JAZZ (HIGH VOICE)** 00843192 ....$16.99	**166. ORNETTE COLEMAN** 00843241 ....$16.99
97. MAYBE I'M AMAZED* 00843148 ....$16.99	**132. STAN GETZ ESSENTIALS** 00843193 ....$16.99	**167. JOHNNY MANDEL** 00103642 ....$16.99
98. DAVE FRISHBERG 00843149 ....$16.99	**133. STAN GETZ FAVORITES** 00843194 ....$16.99	**168. TADD DAMERON** 00103663 ....$16.99
99. SWINGING STANDARDS 00843150 ....$16.99	**134. NURSERY RHYMES*** 00843196 ....$17.99	**169. BEST JAZZ STANDARDS** 00109249 ....$19.99
100. LOUIS ARMSTRONG 00740423 ....$16.99	**135. JEFF BECK** 00843197 ....$16.99	**170. ULTIMATE JAZZ STANDARDS** 00109250 ....$19.99
101. BUD POWELL 00843152 ....$16.99	**136. NAT ADDERLEY** 00843198 ....$16.99	**171. RADIOHEAD** 00109305 ....$16.99
102. JAZZ POP 00843153 ....$16.99	**137. WES MONTGOMERY** 00843199 ....$16.99	**172. POP STANDARDS** 00111669 ....$16.99
103. ON GREEN DOLPHIN STREET & OTHER JAZZ CLASSICS 00843154 ....$16.99	**138. FREDDIE HUBBARD** 00843200 ....$16.99	**174. TIN PAN ALLEY** 00119125 ....$16.99
104. ELTON JOHN 00843155 ....$16.99	**139. JULIAN "CANNONBALL" ADDERLEY** 00843201 ....$16.99	**175. TANGO** 00119836 ....$16.99
105. SOULFUL JAZZ 00843151 ....$16.99	**140. JOE ZAWINUL** 00843202 ....$16.99	**176. JOHNNY MERCER** 00119838 ....$16.99
106. SLO' JAZZ 00843117 ....$16.99	**141. BILL EVANS STANDARDS** 00843156 ....$16.99	**177. THE II-V-I PROGRESSION** 00843239 ....$19.99
107. MOTOWN CLASSICS 00843116 ....$16.99	**142. CHARLIE PARKER GEMS** 00843222 ....$16.99	**178. JAZZ/FUNK** 00121902 ....$16.99
108. JAZZ WALTZ 00843159 ....$16.99	**143. JUST THE BLUES** 00843223 ....$16.99	**179. MODAL JAZZ** 00122273 ....$16.99
109. OSCAR PETERSON 00843160 ....$16.99	**144. LEE MORGAN** 00843229 ....$16.99	**180. MICHAEL JACKSON** 00122327 ....$16.99
110. JUST STANDARDS 00843161 ....$16.99	**145. COUNTRY STANDARDS** 00843230 ....$16.99	**181. BILLY JOEL** 00122329 ....$16.99
111. COOL CHRISTMAS 00843162 ....$16.99	**146. RAMSEY LEWIS** 00843231 ....$16.99	**182. "RHAPSODY IN BLUE" & 7 OTHER CLASSICAL-BASED JAZZ PIECES** 00116847 ....$16.99
112. PAQUITO D'RIVERA – LATIN JAZZ* 48020662 ....$16.99	**147. SAMBA** 00843232 ....$16.99	**183. SONDHEIM** 00126253 ....$16.99
113. PAQUITO D'RIVERA – BRAZILIAN JAZZ* 48020663 ....$19.99	**148. JOHN COLTRANE FAVORITES** 00843233 ....$16.99	**184. JIMMY SMITH** 00126943 ....$16.99
114. MODERN JAZZ QUARTET FAVORITES 00843163 ....$16.99	**149. JOHN COLTRANE – GIANT STEPS** 00843234 ....$16.99	**185. JAZZ FUSION** 00127558 ....$16.99
115. THE SOUND OF MUSIC 00843164 ....$16.99	**150. JAZZ IMPROV BASICS** 00843195 ....$19.99	**186. JOE PASS** 00128391 ....$16.99
116. JACO PASTORIUS 00843165 ....$16.99	**151. MODERN JAZZ QUARTET CLASSICS** 00843209 ....$16.99	**187. CHRISTMAS FAVORITES** 00128393 ....$16.99
117. ANTONIO CARLOS JOBIM – MORE HITS 00843166 ....$16.99	**152. J.J. JOHNSON** 00843210 ....$16.99	**188. PIAZZOLLA – 10 FAVORITE TUNES** 48023253 ....$16.99
118. BIG JAZZ STANDARDS COLLECTION 00843167 ....$27.50	**153. KENNY GARRETT** 00843212 ....$16.99	**189. JOHN LENNON** 00138678 ....$16.99
119. JELLY ROLL MORTON 00843168 ....$16.99	**154. HENRY MANCINI** 00843213 ....$16.99	
120. J.S. BACH 00843169 ....$16.99	**155. SMOOTH JAZZ CLASSICS** 00843215 ....$16.99	
121. DJANGO REINHARDT 00843170 ....$16.99	**156. THELONIOUS MONK – EARLY GEMS** 00843216 ....$16.99	
122. PAUL SIMON 00843182 ....$16.99	**157. HYMNS** 00843217 ....$16.99	
123. BACHARACH & DAVID 00843185 ....$16.99	**158. JAZZ COVERS ROCK** 00843219 ....$16.99	
124. JAZZ-ROCK HORN HITS 00843186 ....$16.99	**159. MOZART** 00843220 ....$16.99	

*These do not include split tracks.

0418

Jazz Instruction & Improvisation

BOOKS FOR ALL INSTRUMENTS FROM HAL LEONARD

AN APPROACH TO JAZZ IMPROVISATION
by Dave Pozzi
Musicians Institute Press
Explore the styles of Charlie Parker, Sonny Rollins, Bud Powell and others with this comprehensive guide to jazz improvisation. Covers: scale choices • chord analysis • phrasing • melodies • harmonic progressions • more.
00695135 Book/CD Pack......................$17.95

THE ART OF MODULATING
FOR PIANISTS AND JAZZ MUSICIANS
by Carlos Salzedo &
Lucile Lawrence
Schirmer
The Art of Modulating is a treatise originally intended for the harp, but this edition has been edited for use by intermediate keyboardists and other musicians who have an understanding of basic music theory. In its pages you will find: table of intervals; modulation rules; modulation formulas; examples of modulation; extensions and cadences; ten fragments of dances; five characteristic pieces; and more.
50490581 ....$19.99

BUILDING A JAZZ VOCABULARY
By Mike Steinel
A valuable resource for learning the basics of jazz from Mike Steinel of the University of North Texas. It covers: the basics of jazz • how to build effective solos • a comprehensive practice routine • and a jazz vocabulary of the masters.
00849911 ....$19.99

THE CYCLE OF FIFTHS
by Emile and Laura De Cosmo
This essential instruction book provides more than 450 exercises, including hundreds of melodic and rhythmic ideas. The book is designed to help improvisors master the cycle of fifths, one of the primary progressions in music. Guaranteed to refine technique, enhance improvisational fluency, and improve sight-reading!
00311114 ....$16.99

THE DIATONIC CYCLE
by Emile and Laura De Cosmo
Renowned jazz educators Emile and Laura De Cosmo provide more than 300 exercises to help improvisors tackle one of music's most common progressions: the diatonic cycle. This book is guaranteed to refine technique, enhance improvisational fluency, and improve sight-reading!
00311115 ....$16.95

EAR TRAINING
by Keith Wyatt,
Carl Schroeder and Joe Elliott
Musicians Institute Press
Covers: basic pitch matching • singing major and minor scales • identifying intervals • transcribing melodies and rhythm • identifying chords and progressions • seventh chords and the blues • modal interchange, chromaticism, modulation • and more.
00695198 Book/Online Audio $24.99

EXERCISES AND ETUDES FOR THE JAZZ INSTRUMENTALIST
by J.J. Johnson
Designed as study material and playable by any instrument, these pieces run the gamut of the jazz experience, featuring common and uncommon time signatures and keys, and styles from ballads to funk. They are progressively graded so that both beginners and professionals will be challenged by the demands of this wonderful music.
00842018 Bass Clef Edition $17.99
00842042 Treble Clef Edition $16.95

JAZZOLOGY
THE ENCYCLOPEDIA OF JAZZ THEORY FOR ALL MUSICIANS
by Robert Rawlins and
Nor Eddine Bahha
This comprehensive resource covers a variety of jazz topics, for beginners and pros of any instrument. The book serves as an encyclopedia for reference, a thorough methodology for the student, and a workbook for the classroom.
00311167 ....$19.99

JAZZ THEORY RESOURCES
by Bert Ligon
Houston Publishing, Inc.
This is a jazz theory text in two volumes. **Volume 1 includes**: review of basic theory • rhythm in jazz performance • triadic generalization • diatonic harmonic progressions and analysis • substitutions and turnarounds • and more.
Volume 2 includes: modes and modal frameworks • quartal harmony • extended tertian structures and triadic superimposition • pentatonic applications • coloring "outside" the lines and beyond • and more.
00030458 Volume 1 ....$39.95
00030459 Volume 2 ....$29.95

JOY OF IMPROV
by Dave Frank
and John Amaral
This book/audio course on improvisation for all instruments and all styles will help players develop monster musical skills! Book One imparts a solid basis in technique, rhythm, chord theory, ear training and improv concepts. **Book Two** explores more advanced chord voicings, chord arranging techniques and more challenging blues and melodic lines. The audio can be used as a listening and play-along tool.
00220005 Book 1 – Book/Online Audio...............$27.99
00220006 Book 2 – Book/Online Audio...............$26.99

THE PATH TO JAZZ IMPROVISATION
by Emile and Laura De Cosmo
This fascinating jazz instruction book offers an innovative, scholarly approach to the art of improvisation. It includes in-depth analysis and lessons about: cycle of fifths • diatonic cycle • overtone series • pentatonic scale • harmonic and melodic minor scale • polytonal order of keys • blues and bebop scales • modes • and more.
00310904 ....$14.99

THE SOURCE
THE DICTIONARY OF CONTEMPORARY AND TRADITIONAL SCALES
by Steve Barta
This book serves as an informative guide for people who are looking for good, solid information regarding scales, chords, and how they work together. It provides right and left hand fingerings for scales, chords, and complete inversions. Includes over 20 different scales, each written in all 12 keys.
00240885 ....$19.99

21 BEBOP EXERCISES
by Steve Rawlins
This book/CD pack is both a warm-up collection and a manual for bebop phrasing. Its tasty and sophisticated exercises will help you develop your proficiency with jazz interpretation. It concentrates on practice in all twelve keys – moving higher by half-step – to help develop dexterity and range. The companion CD includes all of the exercises in 12 keys.
00315341 Book/CD Pack..................................$17.95

HAL•LEONARD®
7777 W. BLUEMOUND RD. P.O. BOX 13819 MILWAUKEE, WI 53213

Visit Hal Leonard online at
www.halleonard.com

Prices, contents & availability
subject to change without notice.

0417